Spirit Beckons

Where we are, Spirit is.

D1537934

Photography and Soul Poetry
by Keith Mounts

To Kerry, my wife and loving companion in our search for bluebirds.

Special thanks to Myrtle Sutphin, Tim Fiocchi, Craig Higgins, Lynne Oakes,
Edie Crane, T.R. Fischer, Ann and Jim Utterback,
and Melanie Jewell for their valuable feedback and ideas.

Introduction

At the beginning of 2014 I decided to devote a year to the creation of one social media posting each day that would combine one of my original photographs with some accompanying words. To find the words I would sit with the image, clear my mind, and wait for inspiration from Spirit. You will see there is always a relationship between the photograph and the words. While I didn't quite reach my goal of one per day, I was content at the end of the year. I received encouraging feedback throughout, including the suggestion of creating a book.

I struggled with what to call the text that accompanied the photography. Then a friend suggested "Soul Poetry." As you explore the book, you might consider initially covering my words to see if your own Soul Poetry comes forth.

More Spirit Beckons can be found at http://spiritbeckons.com. There you can find framable images of some of these pages and others not yet published in book form and additional Soul Poetry with companying photographs.

May you find spirit beckoning you every day.

That which is overlooked
in our routines
becomes vibrant
if given loving attention.

Soft light calms an evening by the lake.
Be gentle with yourself.
Softness is strength in the calm heart.

Miracle: butterflies exist.
Deeper miracle: anything exists.

Live Intensely

When the rare presents itself in fog
and streams of light,
receive the gift with gratitude.

The shared experience of community
reveals a hint of the oneness
we all share.

The Source radiates abundance.

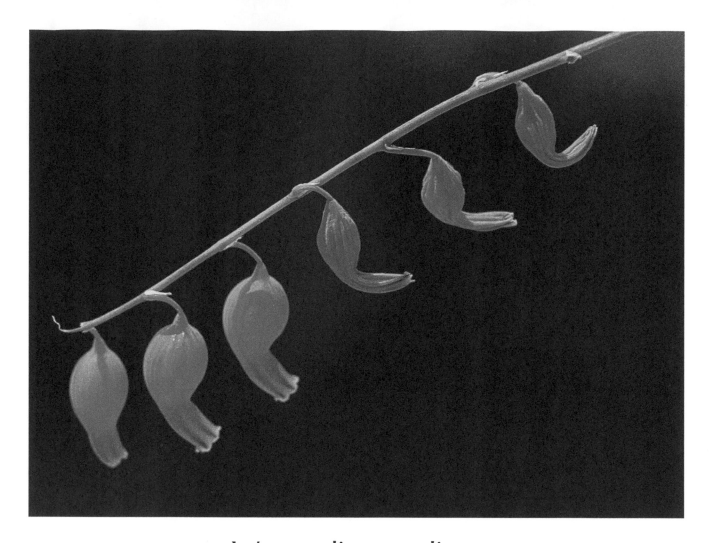

We can live our lives
in expansion or contraction.
One of them
looks better than the other.

The road might be hard,
paved with rough stone.
Even so,
the Light will illuminate the way.

Behind any turmoil,
within any turmoil,
overpowering any turmoil,
is the Light.

In a sometimes crazy and frantic world
we need a place of stability.
The indwelling Spirit of God
is such a place.

Why is a flower so splendid?
Because a Creator made it so,
that it may be joyfully experienced.

Where there is beauty,
there is the Light,
for beauty is drawn to the Light.

When the time comes
and we return to Spirit,
we leave behind a part of ourselves,
floating in memories and love.

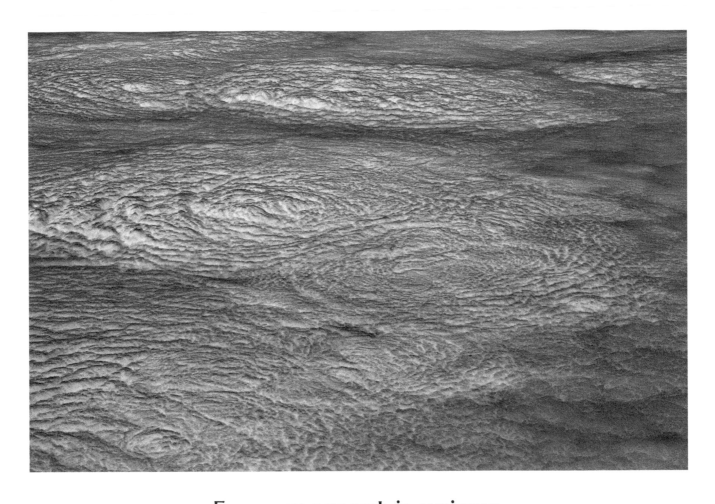

Every moment is unique.
Nothing will ever repeat
in the same way again.
Explore the singular vision
of right now.

Express
in joyous movement,
release fear
in twirling laughter,
savor the freedom
of time forgotten.
Dance.

Share the bounty of creation.
There is always enough.
Lack is an illusion.

Find time for simple pleasures,
like a good perch
from which to view the unfolding Now.

We experience awe, but it fades.
It becomes easy to glance at the sublime,
then return to the highway traffic
and news reports.
Pull over and choose to experience
all the gifts of God.

Express True Self in tranquil water,
and also in raging floods.
We see the reflection of our Soul best
in the quiet calm,
and its manifestation
in the turbulent maelstrom.

Artifacts that defy time and never decay
are those which transcend the physical.
Love, kindness, joy.

Determining the quantum state
of a billion trillion atoms
that were a moment ago uncertain.
This is God's back door
to the universe,
and we are given a key, prayer.

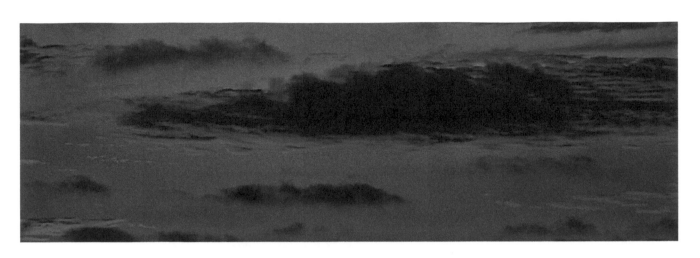

A darkness
can obscure part of the Light,
but never all of it.
Look beyond and around darkness.
Light is always there for us.

Even within a defined path
there is room for unique
expression.

When we experience a loss,
there is always the opportunity
to grow anew
from the place of healing.

In between
every moment
there is a space
to totally change
our future.
It's never too late
to pick a new path
leading to
all the gifts of Spirit.

When it's needed most,
the Light finds us.

In this universe,
to fully experience the Light
we must encounter darkness.

Leave any hate behind.
Let it be covered by debris and vines.
Let the earth reclaim.
Let it disappear.

Flowers and angel wings
at the end of a thorny path.
All roads lead to Spirit,
to God.

Sometimes we think God
is up in the sky,
looking down on us.
God is in the sky, but also inside us,
inside everyone, inside everything.
God IS.

When the surroundings are confusing
and it's hard to figure out
what's going on,
try a different perspective.
Move to your centering place,
where your truth resides.

Lost in the woods?
Pray for a way out
that fulfills
the highest good.
Look carefully,
see the tree cathedral
leading to the Light.

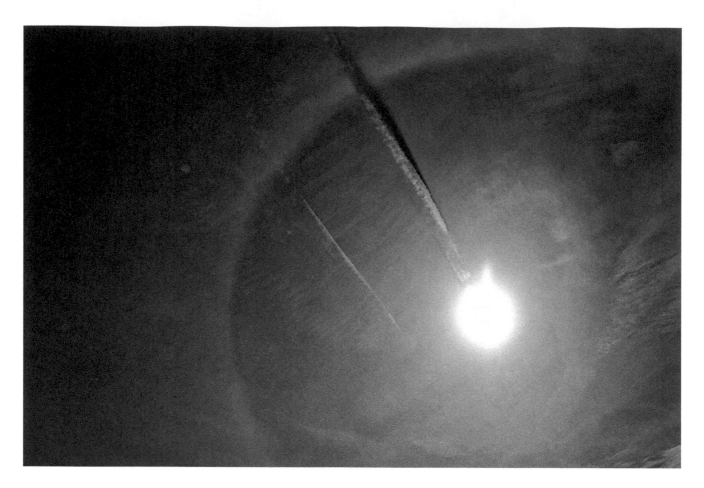

We are each a Soul,
incarnate in a body.
How our minds and bodies
connect to our Soul
resides in the mysteries
of God's creation.

Seek out some morning Light
and be still.
Connect to the moment of creation,
for in the beginning was the Light.

Terrible things happen.
Where is God? In us, co-creating.
Not directly intervening.
If God intervened without our participation,
would we grow in depth of Spirit?
What would our lives mean?

Nothing is ordinary.
Everything, everyone,
is colorful and amazing.
When that isn't your experience,
look closer.
See the hues, the texture,
the manifestation of being.

Even though we all have
aspects of ourselves
that are well formed
and mature,
we also have
the new emerging.
We never stop growing,
for we are eternal.

Encountering the improbable
reminds us that all things
are possible
as co-creators with God.

Remember them
for the beauty they created
in grace and truth.

As we move faster, trees teach permanence,
holding the soil against erosion,
the ages in the rings of their growth,
the wind in their rustling leaves.
Touch a respected tree
and let its wisdom infuse your heart.

There is one thing we can always know
when we take off into the unknown:
Spirit will provide
the adventure, challenges, and sustenance.

Each fragment of our experience
carries a message.
Fill every moment with Love,
the only message assured to align
with God's infinite creation.

When the next phase of the journey is hazy,
mill about with like souls.
Absorb the companionship, learn from each other,
and when the moment arrives,
release the parking brake.

There are ways to see
the higher realms.
Relaxing into the
gifts of Spirit
is one of them.

In what form
will an angel appear in your life?

Live fully in the present
but remember the paths walked with those loved.
Our memories of those now in Spirit
invite their presence.
And we know for a moment
that nothing is ever lost,
only obscured by mortal perception.

Sometimes
we are swept off the ground
we thought to be solid.
But we carry within us
a mighty anchor of stability,
the unbreakable bond
between our true selves
and immutable Spirit.

Look close by for your next blessing.
Sometimes they fill the sky,
but more often they are intimate.

To relax at the end of a stressful day
it may be helpful to rip something up.
As long as the object of your tension relief
is inanimate and expendable,
this is a fine idea.

Spirit provides
transient openings to the Mystery.
Recognize this gift when offered
and embrace the moment.

Life is like a big bowl of flowers.
It's full of beauty
and there's more to it
than we ever expected.

Some days don't start off so well.
Thank Spirit for the blessings of the day,
clean up the mess
and buy a new mailbox.
You see, things are better already.

Some days
need no more accomplishment
than to enjoy the wonder of what is.

Just because it's cracked
doesn't mean it's broken.
Cracks in the Veil
are places of intense healing Light.

Even in the middle of the muck and mud,
there are rainbows.

If you don't know
where you are going,
but the journey is lovely,
the destination finds you.

If built with Love,
guided by Spirit,
there are no limits
on our creation.

Morning dew can get your feet wet
and be jewels of light.
Focus on the light.

We don't know what's coming next.
So be grateful for everything,
and when there are flowers along the way,
say a prayer
for the blessings of beauty.

The edges of perception
are the sentries of Spirit guidance.

Be exuberant in the Light.

Sometimes,
to find our true selves,
we have to experience what is not true for us.
It can be embarrassing.

Be prepared to travel,
unless the end of the road has been reached.
By the way, it hasn't.

Follow the path,
climb the trellis,
but send off some shoots
to find where
there is even more
Light.

Creation is abundant.
What we need is provided,
but we have to perceive the bounty,
then claim it.

Unfoldment devoid of expectation
allows the beauty of the highest good
to emerge.

We don't
have to wait
for an occasional
glimpse of the Light
of Spirit.
The Light
is within us.
Following the path
of the highest good
reveals
our Holy Essence.

Doing can dominate our lives.
Elevate Being.
Return often to your places of peace.

There are bridges over every obstacle.
Unknown is the length of the journey
to find a crossing.

It may seem
we are lightly striding through life,
but the footprints we leave
are larger than we know.
Every choice changes the universe.

We often prefer straight lines.
But this is not nature's way.
We won't learn all the lessons of Spirit
unless we follow the contours of insight.

Be unique.
Be amazing.
Be Love.

We all have
the Light of
Spirit within.
To be seen
we have to allow
the Light to shine.
Turn on your Light.
Be dazzling.

Clover is a happy plant.
Be like a field of clover.
Be really happy!

Agecroft Hall & Gardens

Before striking out on a long journey,
absorb energy
from that which engages connections to Spirit.

Ride gently on the Earth.

We live on a thread in the weave of creation.
When we return to Spirit, we lift off the surface,
and infinite weavings and tapestries are visible,
each unique and incredibly beautiful.

If it appears the ground is coming up fast
and all is lost,
spread your wings.
A gentle landing awaits.

Go over cliffs, survive the plunge.
Looked at from the distance of time,
falls can be a beautiful thing.

Pelicans flying in traffic lanes?
You, too, can do something
oddly unexpected today.

Be uplifted
knowing you are surrounded at all times
by angels of Light.

Wherever you
may be on your
spiritual progression,
it is perfect
when seen
from the Holy,
where eternity
is glimpsed
in its entirety.

A veil covers the details of our life journey.
Seen vaguely are bridges across rivers,
mysterious obstacles,
gateways to the Light.
We are blessed with infinite possibilities
to discover and create.

Many things in our lives
open doors leading to anxiety.
We need places of peace for restoration.
Go there.

Generations are nurtured in a home by a tree.
The gift of the tree, tranquility in constancy.
The gift of families,
laughing children on a swing in the branches.

We think the Light is out there
and try to build structures to reach it.
But our constructions fall short.
Instead, travel within.
The Light awaits our joyous realization.

There is a Light within us.
From inside where we reside
it can be hard to see.
If you want to know how bright it is shining,
look around you for golden reflections.

Life in the divine flow,
always finding a path, never stopping,
being God's love in all places.

Like a galaxy of flowers,
each with divine potential,
we can bloom at any time.
Choose to bloom anew every day.

Honor
that which
has served
you well,
even if it's not
as it once was.

When sunset falls on other worlds,
do souls indwell beings there,
settling into their homes for the night?
Do you dream of distant shores?

Life is an emergent process.
Let your best and most beautiful
come forth again and again.

Inside granite, where we expect total darkness,
stunning colors and details
need light to be seen.
What glory within you
will you bring to the Light?

What lies beyond
our perception?
Infinite possibilities.

Since we are one with God,
what we see is what God sees.
Give God the gift
of looking for
the magnificence of all creation.

Tranquility isn't static.
It has to flow from moment to moment,
always reinforcing itself
as intellect nibbles at the edges,
trying to define
what can only be experienced.

The journey
sometimes requires
trusting bridges
built long ago.

The gift
of a rare and enjoyable sight
may only last a moment,
more likely to be seen
when looking up.

Clouds part to reveal
a distant sea and stunning lands.
There is always more
wonder to be revealed.

CPSIA information can be obtained
at www.ICGtesting.com
Printed in the USA
BVHW021927061220
595051BV00026B/1825